DREAM JOBS IN

TRANSPORTATION, DISTRIBUTION, AND LOGISTICS

CYNTHIA O'BRIEN

CRABTREE
PUBLISHING COMPANY
WWW.CRABTREEBOOKS.COM

CUTTING-EDGE CAREERS IN TECHNICAL EDUCATION

Author:
Cynthia O'Brien

Series research and development:
Reagan Miller

Editorial director:
Kathy Middleton

Editor:
Petrice Custance

Proofreader:
Lorna Notsch

Design, photo research, and prepress:
Katherine Berti

Print and production coordinator:
Katherine Berti

Photographs:
Alamy
Bayne Stanley: p. 22 (bottom left)
iStockphoto
charliemarcos: p. 13 (bottom)
Jacob Wackerhausen: p. 14 (bottom)
ollo: p. 8 (bottom)
Shutterstock
Andrey Khachatryan: p. 26 (bottom)
Angleo Giampiccolo: p. 24 (bottom)
bluefish_ds: p. 4 (center left)
DW labs Incorporated: p. 4 (bottom right)
Eric Buermeyer: p. 18 (bottom right)
FashionStock.com: p. 5 (left model)
Greg K_ca: p. 28 (top background trucks)
John Blanton: p. 13 (top)
JStone: p. 5 (top left)
Julie Cooper: p. 17 (top left)
lev radin: p. 5 (center model)
NAN728: front cover (top left)
Ovidiu Hrubaru: p. 5 (right model)
Ruslan Sitarchuk: front cover (bottom right)
Sheila Fitzgerald: p. 15 (bottom)
Stoyan Yotov: front cover (center)
Tuckraider: p. 21 (center left)
Viappy: p. 8 (center left)
All other images by Shutterstock

Library and Archives Canada Cataloguing in Publication

O'Brien, Cynthia (Cynthia J.), author
Dream jobs in transportation, distribution & logistics / Cynthia O'Brien.
(Cutting-edge careers in technical education)
Includes index.
Issued in print and electronic formats.
ISBN 978-0-7787-4447-4 (hardcover).--
ISBN 978-0-7787-4458-0 (softcover).--
ISBN 978-1-4271-2033-5 (HTML)
1. Transportation--Vocational guidance--Juvenile literature. 2. Transport workers--Training of--Juvenile literature. 3. Industrial management--Vocational guidance--Juvenile literature. I. Title.
HD8039.T7O27 2018 j331.7'61388 C2018-900268-9
C2018-900269-7

Library of Congress Cataloging-in-Publication Data

Names: O'Brien, Cynthia (Cynthia J.), author.
Title: Dream jobs in transportation, distribution & logistics / Cynthia O'Brien.
Description: New York : Crabtree Publishing Company, [2018] | Series: Cutting-edge careers in technical education | Includes index.
Identifiers: LCCN 2018004041 (print) | LCCN 2018005721 (ebook) | ISBN 9781427120335 (Electronic) | ISBN 9780778744474 (hardcover : alk. paper) | ISBN 9780778744580 (pbk. : alk. paper)
Subjects: LCSH: Transportation--Vocational guidance--Juvenile literature.
Classification: LCC HE152 (ebook) | LCC HE152 .O25 2018 (print) | DDC 388.023--dc23
LC record available at https://lccn.loc.gov/2018004041

Crabtree Publishing Company
www.crabtreebooks.com 1-800-387-7650

Printed in the U.S.A./052018/CG20180309

In Canada: We acknowledge the financial support of the Government of Canada through the Canada Book Fund for our publishing activities.

Published in Canada
Crabtree Publishing
616 Welland Ave.
St. Catharines, Ontario
L2M 5V6

Published in the United States
Crabtree Publishing
PMB 59051
350 Fifth Avenue, 59th Floor
New York, New York 10118

Published in the United Kingdom
Crabtree Publishing
Maritime House
Basin Road North, Hove
BN41 1WR

Published in Australia
Crabtree Publishing
3 Charles Street
Coburg North
VIC 3058

CONTENTS

SKILLS FOR THE JOB

Do you love figuring out how something works? Would you like to learn how to craft beautiful jewelry or build a house? The future is very bright for people with the right training.

Taking courses in Career and Technical Education (CTE) can lead you to your dream job! CTE programs combine academic studies, such as math and science, with valuable hands-on training. CTE students develop job-specific skills that are in high demand by employers. The CTE courses available to you will depend on where you live, but most high schools and many middle schools have courses to offer.

To make planning a little easier, there are 16 career clusters within the CTE program. Some examples of CTE clusters are Information Technology, Manufacturing, Arts and Communications, Government and Public Administration, and Architecture and Construction. Each CTE career cluster is divided into job pathways. Each job pathway is a grouping of jobs that require similar interests and paths of study. For example, in the Arts and Communications cluster, the Performing Arts pathway includes jobs such as makeup artist and costume designer, while the Journalism and Broadcasting pathway includes jobs such as writer and reporter.

City managers are in charge of making sure their city's departments all run safely and efficiently, including parks and recreation, fire, police, and transportation.

WHY CTE?

There is a huge and exciting variety of CTE careers. Employers need people who embrace challenge. Such challenges can range from finding clients their dream home to figuring out how an engine works. Students who enjoy solving problems and looking at things in new or different ways are ideal candidates for CTE.

By 2020, about 10 million new skilled workers will be needed in the United States alone. This huge demand means great opportunities for you!

DID YOU KNOW?

SkillsUSA and Skills Canada are organizations that promote career and technical education in middle schools and high schools. They offer annual competitions for students across all CTE clusters at both state/provincial and national levels.

DID YOU KNOW?

On February 3, 2013, the lights went out for 34 minutes during the Super Bowl in New Orleans, Louisiana! Electricians rushed to the rescue and the game continued.

Christian Siriano studied fashion design in college. He then had internships at famous fashion houses Vivienne Westwood and Alexander McQueen before winning the fashion design series Project Runway in 2008.

Carpenters work with wood to build homes, craft furniture, and create works of art. Some **Indigenous** peoples carve totem poles, which are deeply meaningful to their cultures. These stunning totem poles are on display in Stanley Park in Vancouver, Canada.

GET THINGS MOVING!

Get in the fast lane! Transportation jobs focus on getting both people and things moving.

The next time you see an airplane soar overhead or a train whizz by, just think about all the people who keep things—and people—moving. It takes a huge team! You can be part of this team if you want to make a damaged sports car look brand-new, or if you're fascinated by how an airplane works. Maybe you love the idea of working on a ship at sea. In this CTE cluster, technicians and mechanics work on machinery. Meanwhile, drivers and pilots operate vehicles, and many other people work in traffic control, warehouses, and other parts of the industry.

TRANSPORTATION, DISTRIBUTION, AND LOGISTICS JOB PATHWAYS:

TRANSPORTATION OPERATIONS	People in these jobs keep things moving, such as drivers, railroad conductors, and traffic controllers.
LOGISTICS PLANNING AND MANAGEMENT	People are the organizers. They make sure things move smoothly from place to place.
WAREHOUSING AND DISTRIBUTION	Centers are places where goods are stored until needed. These centers need people to receive, pack, load, and ship out the goods.
FACILITY AND MOBILE EQUIPMENT MAINTENANCE	These jobs include aircraft mechanics, ship repairers, and others whose job it is to ensure everything works efficiently.
TRANSPORTATION SYSTEMS	Employees manage the movement of people and things, such as air traffic control. Other jobs include planners who design routes and inspectors who make sure things run smoothly.
HEALTH, SAFETY, AND ENVIRONMENTAL MANAGEMENT	People in these careers work to make transportation systems safe and clean for the population and the environment.
SALES AND SERVICE	Workers rent cars, arrange travel, sell vehicles, and more.

HOW TO USE THIS BOOK

Each two-page spread focuses on a specific career in the Transportation, Distribution, and **Logistics** CTE cluster. For each career, you will find a detailed description of life on the job, advice on the best educational path to take (see right), and tips on what you can do now to begin preparing for your dream job.

A CHANCE TO EXPLORE

The job pathways in CTE clusters help you keep your options open. You can think about what interests you and explore what is out there. Some colleges offer discovery programs, so you can find out what job might be the right fit for you. There are also CTE summer camps, online quizzes, and skill competitions, such as the Career Pathways Showcase. Just remember, you do not have to choose one career right now. Let's get started!

Car salespeople are good communicators who like working with people. They must be knowledgeable about different car models to give the best advice to their customers.

YOUR PATH

SECONDARY SCHOOL

This section lists the best subjects to take in high school.

POST-SECONDARY

Some jobs require an **apprenticeship** and **certification** while others require a college or university degree. This section gives you an idea of the best path to take after high school.

Inventory managers need to know what is in a warehouse at all times. Data **software** helps them keep track of items.

DID YOU KNOW?

Transportation YOU is a mentoring program for girls ages 13–18 who may be interested in a career in the transportation industry. It offers career development programs, social events, leadership training, internships, and scholarships.

AUTOMOTIVE SERVICE TECHNICIAN

Combine car smarts and tech skills to keep vehicles running smoothly.

An alternative fuel vehicle (AFV) technician works on cars that use **ethanol** or other **renewable** fuels.

Crazy about cars? North Americans buy millions of cars each year, and each one will need a repair or service at some point. This is where an automotive service technician comes in. This expert learns all about cars and light trucks so he or she can **diagnose** a problem when something goes wrong. Technicians use special, computerized equipment to pinpoint issues with a car's electronic or mechanical workings and parts.

DID YOU KNOW?

Technological **innovations** mean that the job of an automotive service technician is always changing. There are always new things to learn, such as constantly advancing computer systems in cars. There are also electric cars, **hybrid** cars, and cars that run on alternative fuels, such as ethanol. There are even cars that drive themselves! What could be next?

In February 2018, BMW of North America launched an automotive service technician training program for veterans. Located right on the Camp Pendleton military base in California, the 16-week program prepares soldiers for a career outside the army. BMW needs more technicians who are specially trained to work on its vehicles.

ON THE JOB

Figuring out the problem is just the start of a technician's job. After testing, she or he can get to work on repairs, replacements, or servicing. The service technician works on braking and steering systems, heating and air conditioning, engines, and more. There may also be oil changes or tire rotations to do. In larger car repair shops, automotive technicians may specialize. There might be a brake repair technician, for example, or tune-up technicians who focus on fuel systems.

YOUR PATH TO WORK AS AN AUTOMOTIVE SERVICE TECHNICIAN

SECONDARY SCHOOL

CTE courses, such as auto servicing and mechanics. Computer, math, and science courses are also helpful.

POST-SECONDARY

Auto service college programs lead to certification. Many auto companies offer workplace training for their specific vehicles.

Many repairs need to be done from underneath a car. A car lift supports the vehicle so that technicians have a safe space to work.

WHAT CAN YOU DO NOW?

Start researching different kinds of cars, both on how they work and how they are made. Visit car shows to see different makes and models up close. Try riding go-karts or dirt bikes to get a feel for how they operate. Some car clubs offer junior driving days for kids ages 12 and older.

DID YOU KNOW?

Gas-powered cars account for 20 percent of the world's carbon **emissions**, which are a major cause of climate change. Some countries, such as India and Norway, plan to ban gas-powered cars in favor of electric or hybrid cars by 2030.

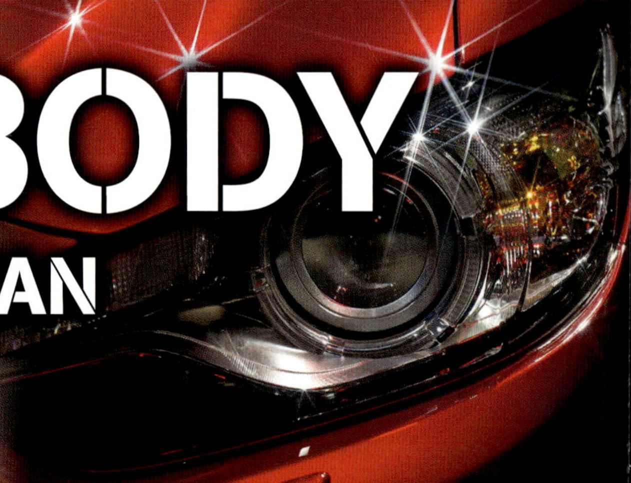

AUTO BODY REPAIR TECHNICIAN

You can make cars look good as new.

Road and other accidents happen. Some are minor, leaving small dents and scratches. Others might cause major damage. Auto body repair technicians know just what to do. Technicians use problem-solving skills and great attention to detail to assess the damage and make a repair plan. This might include fitting a new door panel or hood or replacing a bumper. Although repairers concentrate on damage to the outside and frame of the car, with newer cars, technicians need to access a car's computer systems to ensure everything is operating properly.

ON THE JOB

Most technicians work in an auto body repair shop, but they may find a job with a car dealership. They deal with customers, so good people skills are very helpful. But a technician's main job is working on cars. This includes working with different materials, including metal, plastic, and fiberglass, so **welding** tools, metal cutters, and **hydraulic** jacks are all part of a technician's equipment. Specific repairs may need specialist technicians. Automotive painters ensure a perfect finish. Glass replacement experts often deal with broken windshields.

Painting a car requires a painting booth and spray painting equipment. Painters wear full, protective clothing and a mask.

WHAT CAN YOU DO NOW?

Get to know how cars are made by studying their different parts and components. Research the latest technology being installed in cars. Learn how to take apart and put back together a piece of machinery. Search online for kid-friendly projects or experiments with machinery or electronics. See if there are any car clubs for kids in your area.

Newer technology in vehicles is changing the knowledge auto body repair technicians need. They must be able to diagnose problems with and restore all technology in cars—from the safety systems to the entertainment systems.

DID YOU KNOW?

The Margaret Dunning Foundation provides grants to CTE programs in the Transportation cluster. Margaret Dunning was a lifelong car lover who did much of her own auto body repair. She was still driving her prized 1930 Packard 740 Roadster in car shows at the age of 103!

YOUR PATH TO WORK AS AN AUTO BODY REPAIR TECHNICIAN

SECONDARY SCHOOL

CTE courses teach basic auto body repair, including refinishing work.

POST-SECONDARY

An apprenticeship program will lead to certification.

DID YOU KNOW?

The Collision Repair Education Foundation offers grants and scholarships to CTE students. It also hosts career fairs for high school and college students.

When replacing parts of a damaged car, a technician must weld new pieces of sheet metal to the rest of the car.

MOTORCYCLE TECHNICIAN

Fast-moving two-wheelers need specialized care.

If the sound of a finely tuned, revving motorcycle gives you a thrill, your future might be in motorcycle repair. Many owners are passionate about their motorbikes, but many do not have the expertise to repair them. Technicians understand the many types of motorcycle engines, from the **single cylinder** on a dirt bike to much more complicated sport bike engines. They diagnose problems, repair electrical systems, and replace parts on all makes and models.

DID YOU KNOW?

If superfast motorcycles are your passion, you might think about a job working as part of a race team. Get your college training, and then try to get an apprenticeship working as part of the team. Work your way up, and you could be the technician behind the winning machine!

Technicians need a motorcycle driving license. A test drive helps them diagnose problems with bikes that need repair.

Technicians travel with race teams to national and international events. At a pit stop, technicians have only seconds to change a tire or refuel the bike.

Motorcycles are going green! Electric motorcycles run fully on electricity. The power is stored in a rechargeable battery that operates the motor.

YOUR PATH TO WORK AS A MOTORCYCLE MECHANIC

SECONDARY SCHOOL

Automotive CTE courses, as well as science and technology courses are extremely valuable

POST-SECONDARY

Some companies, such as Honda and Harley-Davidson, offer apprenticeship programs for their specific vehicles.

ON THE JOB

Motorcycle technicians are prepared to work on classic motorbikes with traditional engines and on the latest makes with computerized systems. Many technicians also have the training to work on snowmobiles and all-terrain vehicles (ATVs). A typical day may be maintenance work, such as oil changes and tire checks, but sometimes an entire engine rebuild might be needed. After the repairs are made, a test drive is a must to make sure everything is running smoothly and safely.

WHAT CAN YOU DO NOW?

Learn how engines operate. Research how the design of a motorcyle can affect its speed. See if any local riding clubs have programs for junior riders. Honda sometimes offers junior racers programs for kids ages 6–12.

ABLE SEAFARER

A career at sea is a thrilling and challenging job.

A ship is an exciting, active place to work, and operating such a large vessel takes a dedicated team. From engineers to ordinary seafarers, each has his or her job to do. An able seafarer is one grade higher than an ordinary seafarer, or deckhand. During training, students take various courses, including **navigation**. It takes three years of experience to qualify as an "unlimited able seafarer." But that's not all. He or she must have worked on an ocean-going vessel. After this training, an unlimited able seafarer is qualified to work on any vessel, regardless of size. There is a huge shortage of qualified able seafarers, so applicants are in high demand.

ON THE JOB

Able seafarers work on **commercial** ships, recreational ships, and for the coast guard. On board, able seafarers must know how to operate deck and cargo machinery. Their work also includes operating **mooring** equipment, such as ropes and anchors, to hold the ship at the dock. As well as these regular jobs, an able seafarer understands emergency and other safety procedures, such as first aid. Another important task is maintaining and operating the lifesaving equipment.

DID YOU KNOW?

The Disabled Sailing Association of Ontario (DSAO) is an organization based in Toronto, Canada that provides sailing opportunities for differently abled people. Programs range from providing relaxed days at sea to offering sailing certification training and running competitive **regattas**.

Keeping watch on the bridge is an important duty to ensure the ship is on course and to look out for other vessels.

WHAT CAN YOU DO NOW?

Learn all you can about the mechanics of a ship. Take a first aid course. See if you can take a boat or ferry ride to experience life at sea. Enquire if any sailing clubs in your area have programs or activities for kids. KidShip Sailing School, located on Chesapeake Bay in Maryland, offers sailing lessons for kids ages 5 to 15.

YOUR PATH TO WORK AS AN ABLE SEAFARER

SECONDARY SCHOOL

Courses in science, geography, and math will be most beneficial.

POST-SECONDARY

The U.S. Coast Guard issues a Merchant Mariner's Credential. Transport Canada oversees the Bridge Watch training program and certification.

A ship's crew practices firefighting procedures to make sure they are ready in an emergency.

Shipping is the most energy-efficient way to transport large amounts of goods. But ships create pollution through carbon and other emissions. The global shipping industry is working to make ships more environmentally friendly. One surprising way is to use a certain type of paint around the ship's **hull** that helps the ship move more easily through the water, reducing emissions.

TRAFFIC, SHIPPING, AND RECEIVING CLERKS

Demand is high around the world for shipped goods.

Warehouses are places that store goods or materials. Many companies store goods, such as furniture, in warehouses until customers buy them. Companies also have distribution centers to send goods to different **retailers** or customers. Online retailers do not have traditional stores. Instead, they receive and send their merchandise, or goods for sale, from warehouses and distribution centers. Who keeps track of all this movement? Clerks! These organized recordkeepers maintain an inventory of all the goods or materials that arrive and leave a warehouse.

ON THE JOB

In a large warehouse, there are specialized clerks. Receiving clerks accept the goods at the warehouse. They may have come from the factory that made them, for example. At the warehouse, the clerk checks the goods for damage and arranges for them to be stored. The shipping clerk is responsible for sending the goods from the warehouse or distribution center. This clerk must pack and label the goods and attach bills or other shipping forms. A traffic clerk will receive goods, keep records, and oversee the transportation of goods out of the warehouse.

Before goods are shipped or when they arrive, shipping forms must be checked by clerks to make sure weights, charges, and all other information is correct.

WHAT CAN YOU DO NOW?

Get organized! Employers need organized people who have a good eye for detail. Start practicing by choosing contents in an area of your house, such as your kitchen pantry. Make an **itemized** list of the inventory and then try keeping track of what goes out and what comes in for an entire week. Try putting your data into a computerized spreadsheet.

Amazon, the world's largest online retailer, will hire as many as 50,000 new people when it opens its second North American headquarters.

Customer service is often part of a clerk's job, including dealing with customer complaints and questions.

YOUR PATH TO WORK AS A TRAFFIC, SHIPPING, OR RECEIVING CLERK

SECONDARY SCHOOL

Math and computer courses are essential.

POST-SECONDARY

Most people learn on the job after finishing high school. However, you may consider college courses in warehousing and logistics.

DID YOU KNOW?

Online shopping is on the increase all over the world. In 2016, global online sales were $1.9 trillion. By 2020, sales are expected to be more than $4 trillion. To keep up with demand, companies are building more and larger warehouses to store goods.

A computerized inventory system helps clerks keep track of the inventory coming in and going out.

RAILROAD CONDUCTOR

A conductor keeps trains on the right track.

The first trains in the United States started carrying passengers and **freight** more than 180 years ago. Today, railroad tracks crisscross North America, and millions of people take the train. A railroad conductor is in charge of the safe operation of a train and its crew members. Conductors make sure passengers and freight arrive safely and on time. They also oversee other train workers, such as switching crews who help move train cars. Sometimes, there is more than one conductor. A conductor who works on trains is called a road service conductor. Yard conductors work in the **rail yard**.

ON THE JOB

If you've traveled on a train, a conductor may have collected your ticket, but that is only part of the conductor's job. He or she keeps track of schedules, making sure trains leave and arrive on time. The conductor inspects the train and arranges for repairs. On freight trains, the conductor oversees loading and unloading of **cargo**. In the rail yard, a conductor makes sure that freight trains are carrying the correct cargo. Conductors take charge in emergency situations, too, such as a train going off the tracks or bad weather, or if a train must take another route.

Women in the railroad industry are often called "women of steel."

On the journey, conductors communicate with other rail crew about any changes, such as timing and stops.

WHAT CAN YOU DO NOW?

Learn all you can about trains, such as how they are made and how they work. Search online for videos showing railroad conductors on the job. Study your local railway timetables and routes.

MEET A RAILWAY CONDUCTOR

As a teenager, Kassie Cleary didn't travel on trains, but she heard them rolling down the track near her home in New York State. Today, Kassie not only travels on trains, she is in charge of their movements. She is a passenger conductor for Amtrak. The train will not go or stop without her okay. To qualify as a conductor, Kassie trained for eight weeks. Among many other things, she learned the rule books for each of the territories in which she would travel. Each one is different. After training, Kassie followed crew on these routes. Traveling is one of the things she loves most about her job. Kassie spends much of her time on the move, and considers her coworkers her "railroad family." Meeting new people also makes her job special. For Kassie, being a conductor means that every day is a fresh new journey—in more ways than one!

YOUR PATH TO WORK AS A RAILWAY CONDUCTOR

SECONDARY SCHOOL

Computer and electronics courses are a great start.

POST-SECONDARY

Many colleges offer a Railroad Conductor program. You will also need on-the-job training.

DID YOU KNOW?

Under the U.S. Department of Transportation, the Federal Railroad Association (FRA) oversees railroad conductor certification in the United States. Transport Canada and the Railway Association of Canada (RAC) regulate training courses in Canada.

Freight train conductors are responsible for goods instead of people. They maintain the transportation records for the freight and make sure trains arrive safely to their destinations.

RESERVATION, TRAVEL, AND TRANSPORT AGENTS

Be a go-to person for travel planning!

Do you have a passion for travel? Do you enjoy working with people? Consider a career as a travel agent! Millions of people travel every day. Some travel for business, while others go on vacation or travel to see family, friends, and to attend events. There are many details to work out, from schedules and fees to picking just the right vacation spot. Agents help people get where they need to go.

Agents work to get their clients the lowest price possible for their vacation. They often have access to deals that clients cannot normally get themselves.

ON THE JOB

Travel agencies, airlines, and bus and railway companies all employ travel agents. Using the computerized **network** Global Distribution System (GDS), agents get the information they need to do their job. This includes booking hotel rooms, making travel bookings, and arranging car rentals for individuals, families, and large groups. Agents are also travel advisers for their customers. They spend a lot of time talking to people about vacation or other destinations and the costs involved. They often help to plan **itineraries** and supply information about **visas**, passports, and other travel documents.

In an airport, reservation agents help passengers check their bags. They also help young children and other people who need assistance board the plane.

DID YOU KNOW?

If you work as an agent for an airline, you may get free or very low-cost travel for you and your family!

WHAT CAN YOU DO NOW?

The next time you take a trip with family or your school, take note of all the people who help you on your journey. Start reading about other cities and countries around the world. Study local bus, rail, and flight timetables. Plan a full day of activities for you and a friend. Write out each step you will need to take to make your day successful.

YOUR PATH TO WORK AS A RESERVATION, TRAVEL, OR TRANSPORT AGENT

SECONDARY SCHOOL

Math and computer courses are essential. Some high schools offer travel and tourism courses.

POST-SECONDARY

College programs range from six months to two years. Many courses are online. Certification varies depending on where you live.

Agents advise their clients on how to have an incredible time as they travel around the world. It is important for agents to be knowledgeable about the cultures and customs of different countries and to share that information with their clients.

DID YOU KNOW?

The American Society of Travel Agents (ASTA) offers certification in the United States. In Canada, you can become a Certified Travel Counsellor by passing an exam given by the Association of Canadian Travel Agents (ACTA).

AVIATION MAINTENANCE TECHNICIAN

You can keep aircraft flying high.

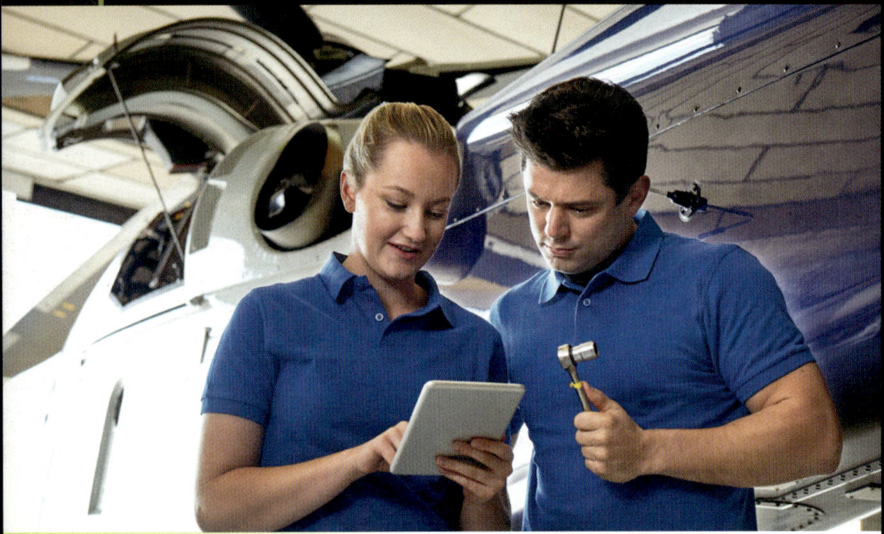

Thousands of airplanes take to the skies every day. Before they can take off, the maintenance crew issues a Certificate of Release to Service. This confirms that an airplane is safe to fly.

Indigenous students in the aircraft maintenance engineering program at the Saskatchewan Indian Institute of Technologies in Canada train on a variety of aircraft. A Sikorsky S-76A helicopter was recently given to the school by the Royal Canadian Air Force.

Take your career to the skies with a job as an **aviation** maintenance technician! Technicians are vital to the aviation industry because they make sure that airplanes and helicopters are safe to fly. A 2016 report from Transport Canada warns of a severe shortage of aviation maintenance technicians in Canada, the United States, and other parts of the world. Today, the Federal Aviation Administration (FAA) in the United States, Transport Canada, and aviation companies have programs, such as student work placements, to encourage the next generation of aviation maintenance technicians. This could be you!

DID YOU KNOW?

Even in the 21st century, few women think about a career in aviation. Groups such as Women in Aviation International, the Association for Women in Aviation Maintenance (AWAM) in the United States, and Elevate Aviation in Canada are working to change this.

ON THE JOB

Aviation maintenance technicians spend their days checking, maintaining, and repairing small and large airplanes and helicopters. Working in a **hangar** or outside, technicians repair and replace wings and other parts. Some people specialize in a particular aircraft or part of an aircraft, such as the hydraulic system. Technicians also do emergency repairs. Many aviation maintenance technicians work on private or commercial aircraft, while others work for the military.

WHAT CAN YOU DO NOW?

Start learning about electrical and computer systems. Research how airplanes work and the systems that run them. Search online for safe-for-kids experiments with electronics. Check to see if there are any mechanics or aviation clubs for kids in your area. If there aren't, think about starting your own club.

YOUR PATH TO WORK AS AN AVIATION MAINTENANCE TECHNICIAN

SECONDARY SCHOOL

Classes in computers, mechanics, and electronics will help prepare you for a college course in aviation mechanics.

POST-SECONDARY

A college degree is required. In the U.S., the FAA issues exams for certification. In Canada, Transport Canada issues certification.

DID YOU KNOW?

Technicians use x-ray equipment to find even the tiniest cracks that could affect an aircraft's safety.

Aviation maintenance competitions offer high school students the chance to test their skills and meet people already working in the field.

AIR TRAFFIC CONTROLLER

Help police the sky's highways.

Every day, more than two-and-a-half million people travel by air in the United States alone. At any one time, thousands of airplanes are in the air. Without traffic lights or actual roads, pilots rely on air traffic controllers to guide them on the highways in the sky. Controllers also guide aircraft on the ground, ensuring that taxiways and runways are clear and safe. Most controllers work in air traffic control towers at airports and in air route traffic control centers. In the United States, some controllers work for the Air Traffic Control Systems Command Center which oversees the air space.

ON THE JOB

On a typical day, air traffic controllers monitor the movement of airplanes with the latest in radar and computer technology. Other specialists, such as traffic management coordinators, also work with controllers to help manage the flow of aircraft traffic. Communication is key to a controller's job. She or he stays in touch with aircraft pilots to supply information, such as instructions for takeoff and landing. Sometimes, for example, a runway may not be free, so a pilot must wait to land. Controllers also supply information on wind, altitude, and weather changes. As they manage the air traffic, controllers stay ready for emergencies, such as dangerous weather conditions.

Most controllers cannot see the aircraft they are managing. Once a plane is in the air, controllers use tracking systems to keep the sky traffic clear.

WHAT CAN YOU DO NOW?

Research how aircraft work. Study how weather patterns affect flight. Learn common aviation terms and the language that air traffic controllers use. This job requires excellent communication skills, especially in stressful situations. Ask friends to set up pretend scenarios with you giving clear and calm instructions while a lot of noise and distraction is happening around you. Practice makes perfect!

MEET AN AIR TRAFFIC CONTROLLER

After taking a tour of the control room in an airport, Kendra Kincade knew she wanted to become a controller. Today, she works at the Edmonton airport in Alberta, Canada, and she couldn't be happier. She loves her fast-paced, challenging career. Every day, Kendra directs the traffic of hundreds of airplanes and helicopters. Constantly changing wind and weather means no day is the same. Kendra needs to think quickly and pay close attention to these changes, so she can instruct pilots to alter their speed, flight paths, or altitudes. As an enthusiastic aviation professional, Kendra wants more people, particularly women, to join her in the industry. To help support women interested in an aviation career, she founded Elevate Aviation. The organization promotes and supports women through grants, mentoring, and more.

DID YOU KNOW?

In the U.S., colleges offer programs approved by the FAA. In Canada, training leads to a license from Transport Canada, but NAV CANADA owns and operates the air traffic towers and control centers.

YOUR PATH TO WORK AS AN AIR TRAFFIC CONTROLLER

SECONDARY SCHOOL

Math, science, and computer science are all good high school foundation courses.

POST-SECONDARY

A college or university degree and up to five years of intensive on-the-job training are required.

DID YOU KNOW?

The Daytona Beach campus of Embry-Riddle Aeronautical University recently added the latest high-tech **consoles** and **simulation** software to its air traffic management student lab.

Controllers have to think about aircraft size when clearing planes for departure. A large airplane will cause a lot of **turbulence** for a small craft behind it.

AVIONICS TECHNICIAN

This career is on the cutting edge of electronics.

Avionics technicians have the dream job of working on the latest navigation and communications systems. They make sure that these systems are working properly and keep up with any new developments. Technicians understand computers, but they must be mechanically minded, as well. They use hand and power tools to repair and replace parts. Avionics technicians are excellent problem solvers. If something goes wrong on a flight, technicians analyze the flight data to identify the problem and fix it.

Bombardier, the world's leading airplane manufacturer, has a new technician training program called Smart Training. Technicians can attend training centers located in Dallas, Texas, or Montreal, Canada, where aircraft simulators keep technicians updated on the very latest technological systems.

ON THE JOB

Generally, avionics technicians take one of two career paths, though sometimes these paths cross. Many technicians are involved in regular inspection and maintenance. At airfields and hangars, they test and repair systems, assemble controls, and install computer software. This work is crucial for the safe operation of any aircraft. Other avionics technicians work in the development stage of new electronics equipment. They think about problems that might occur and use their specialized knowledge and training to inspect and test the new systems before they are used on actual flights.

WHAT CAN YOU DO NOW?

Start learning about airplane design and electronics. Research the electrical systems of airplanes. Search online for flight simulations you can try. Check to see if there are any electronics or aviation clubs for kids in your area. If there aren't, think about starting one of your own at school.

DID YOU KNOW?

Each year the General Aviation Manufacturers Association (GAMA) sponsors the Aviation Design Challenge for high schools. Entrants receive flight simulation software. They must modify the design of an airplane and compete in a virtual fly-off.

YOUR PATH TO WORK AS AN AVIONICS TECHNICIAN

SECONDARY SCHOOL

Courses in computer science, math, mechanics, and electronics will help prepare you for specialized college avionics programs.

POST-SECONDARY

Some colleges offer a blended program of Avionics and Aviation Maintenance. After on-the-job training, the FAA and Transport Canada issue certification.

Testing an airplane's equipment is essential. Technicians read test results and adjust the plane's system settings as necessary.

Some avionics technicians work at NASA's research center and other organizations where cutting-edge research is done.

LOGISTICIAN

These planners make things move.

If you like planning and organizing, you might consider a job as a logistician. These key players make sure that materials, goods, or people get from one place to another. They oversee various jobs in the **supply chain** of a product and can work in many different industries. Logisticians are in high demand because many industries need them, but there are not enough certified people. Logisticians work with clients, so being a good communicator can be very helpful.

ON THE JOB

Logisticians have many responsibilities, including purchasing and arranging transportation. Their workplace might be a factory, an office, or a warehouse, because logisticians are involved in moving everything from military supplies to people. They use computer programs to plan, track, and manage this movement. They also look for ways to improve the time or cost involved in moving things or people. When problems occur in the supply chain, logisticians work out what to do to get things moving again.

DID YOU KNOW?

In 2015, the United States transportation system moved 43.9 million tons (39.8 million metric tons) of freight every day. Logisitians helped to make this happen.

Logistics is vital to protecting the environment. The Transportation industry is a huge source of pollution. Logisticians are planning ways to keep supply chains moving in sustainable ways. For example, the worldwide shipping company FedEx has introduced a program called Eco-Driving. FedEx couriers are taught better driving habits to reduce harmful carbon emissions, such as gentle acceleration and reduced **idling** times.

Drones are revolutionizing logistics. They are being used for direct-to-customer deliveries and to track inventory. They are even being used for warehouse security. Drones can monitor places **stationary** cameras cannot.

WHAT CAN YOU DO NOW?

Logistics is knowing how to get things from point A to point B in a safe and timely manner. Start studying road and highway maps. Get to know your local bus, rail, and flight transportation routes. Create logistics challenges for yourself, such as what would be the most efficient way to get a rock band and all its equipment from London, England to New York City in time for the next show. Get planning!

DID YOU KNOW?

The International Society of Logistics and the American Production and Inventory Control Society (APICS) provide certification programs. The first level is a Demonstrated Logistician and the most senior is the Certified Professional Logistician (CPL).

YOUR PATH TO WORK AS A LOGISTICIAN

SECONDARY SCHOOL

Math and data management courses are essential.

POST-SECONDARY

A college diploma in logistics and business management is required. More senior logistician jobs often require a university degree.

During disasters such as hurricanes and wildfires, logisticians plan how to get aid workers, equipment, and essential supplies to the scene as quickly as possible.

LEARNING MORE

BOOKS

Yuan, Katharine. *Getting a Job in the Transportation Industry.* Rosen, 2016.

Career Companion: Transportation, Distribution, and Logistics. McGraw-Hill, 2011.

Careers in Focus: Transportation. Infobase, 2007.

WEBSITES

WWW.ONTONLINE.OGR This website is a careers resource and includes job descriptions, education requirements, and much more.

WWW.CTSOS.ORG The national council for the Career and Technical Student organizations.

HTTPS://SKILLUSA.ORG This site offers resources and information on competitions, conferences, and other activities.

GLOSSARY

apprenticeship A period of time spent learning skilled work with hands-on training

aviation The operation of aircraft

avionics The development and production of electronic devices for aviation

cargo The goods that are transported by ships, airplanes, trains, or vehicles

certification Certificate that shows someone has achieved a certain level of skill and knowledge

commercial Concerned with business or trade

console A panel of switches used to control an electrical device

diagnose Identify a problem

emissions Substances released into the air

ethanol A type of alcohol that can be used as a clean-burning fuel source

freight Goods carried by trains, trucks, airplanes, or ships

hangar A building where aircraft are kept

hull The frame or body of a ship

hybrid A car with a gasoline engine and electric motor

hydraulic Operated using the pressure of a fluid such as oil

idle To keep the engine of a vehicle running when it is not being driven

Indigenous The original occupants of a land

innovation A new idea, invention, or way of doing things

inventory An itemized list of goods owned

itemized A detailed listing of individual items

itinerary Places to go on a journey

logistics Managing and organizing the movement of goods and people

mooring A place where a vessel can be secured in place

navigation Finding the way to get to a place

network A system of computers connected by communication lines

rail yard An area with a network of railroad tracks used for storing, loading, and unloading rail cars

regatta A sporting event consisting of boat or yacht races

renewable Able to be replaced naturally

retailer A person or business that sells things to a consumer

simulation To imitate the operation of a process or system

single cylinder A basic engine common to motorcycles and scooters

software Programs that are added to a computer system

stationary Does not move

supply chain The system that moves a product from a supplier to a consumer

turbulence A violent or unsteady movement of air or water

visa An official stamp or mark in a passport that allows a person to enter or leave a country

weld To join pieces of metal together by heating and melting

INDEX